Also by Frances M. Koh

Korean Holidays & Festivals

English-Korean Picture Dictionary

Creative Korean Cooking

Oriental Children in American Homes

Adopted from Asia

How It Feels to Grow Up
in
America

FRANCES M. KOH

EastWest Press
Minneapolis • Minnesota

EastWest Press
P.O. Box 14149
Minneapolis, MN 55414

Library of Congress Catalog Card Number 93-72354
International Standard Book Number: 0-9606090-6-7

Text design by Frances M. Koh
Typeset by TypeCetera, Inc., Minneapolis, MN

Printed in the United States of America
FIRST EDITION
10 9 8 7 6 5 4 3 2 1

ACKNOWLEDGEMENT

Special thanks to Betty Schendel, Pat Sparks, Betsy Norum, for putting me in touch with the first few adopted persons who further led me to others; most of all, the unnamed adopted persons who generously shared their experiences with me for this book; Margaret Young, Evelyn Iverson, and Rosemary Wallner, for their helpful suggestions and assistance with copy editing; lastly, but not least, numerous friends who have offered constant support and encouragement for this project.

DEDICATION

This book is dedicated to the eleven adopted persons who generously shared their adoption experiences with me for this book, so that others may learn and understand how it feels to be adopted from Asia and grow up in America.

DISCLAIMER

The materials presented in this book were obtained by tape-recorded interviews with those persons who participated in this study. To insure their privacy, all identifiable information–names, places, personal and family details–have been deleted or altered. Yet some readers may believe they recognize individuals. However, their resemblance, if any, to persons they know may be entirely coincidental.

The drawings of Asian faces on the cover were produced from photos of Asian persons, but they do not represent any of the adopted persons whose experiences are presented in this book.

CONTENTS

PREFACE

After the publication of *Oriental Children in American Homes: How Do They Adjust?* in 1981, many adoptive parents of Korean-born children wrote urging me to write a book dealing with the adoptees' feelings of being adopted and being Asian American.

Needless to say, these concerns are central to the adoptees' experience. Owing to my experience as an adoption worker in the 1960s and having lived in the States for the better part of my life, I've been interested in exploring these concerns for many years. During the past 20 years or more, my interest and knowledge in intercountry adoption, particularly that of involving children from Korea, have continually grown and eventually led me to research and write my first book, *Oriental Children in American Homes* in 1981. Since then, a number of books have been published on the subject of intercountry adoption, but no book has been written from the adoptees' point of view, dealing with the issues facing them in adolescence and young adulthood. This book that features the life stories of eleven adoptees is an attempt to do that.

Being adopted and being Asian-American invite conflicting elements in the adoptees' lives. What kind of conflicts or struggles have they faced? How do they feel about being adopted from Korea and growing up in America?

With these questions in mind, I decided to explore what I consider the most critical areas of the adoptee's experiences, such as the trauma of separation and loss, parental love and support, concerns about birthparents, racial prejudice, friends and dating, ethnic identity, and self-esteem. I then formulated questions designed to bring out their experiences in these areas. Armed with a long list of questions, I set out to find potential interviewees for this project. Finding them was not easy, but eventually, over the years, I found eleven adoptees, ages 14 to 23, who were willing to be interviewed. They were all adopted by Euro-American parents in the 1970s. While four participants were teenagers, the rest were young adults in their early 20s. The names given in the text of the adoptees' accounts are pseudonyms to ensure their privacy.

The result of my interviews have produced a mass of material about each adoptee's experiences. My task, as author of this book, has been to sort out the material and organize it in a coherent logical order, as well as edit or rewrite it—so as to render clarity and understanding of their experiences.

On reading their experiences, one quickly learns that all

adoptees came from different backgrounds and had different experiences in their adoptive homes. Most of them grew up feeling comfortable being adopted and growing up in their American homes. Regardless, they have all faced the issues of racial prejudice and struggled with identity questions.

When they were young and being surrounded by Caucasians, most of them identified with Caucasian features of their parents and friends and, at one time or another, wished they looked like them. In their desire to be all-American, some felt uneasy about their Asian features or felt ambivalent toward their country or people of origin. A few became oblivious to their Asian features and thought they had become Caucasian—probably they became so, in terms of their values and attitudes, if not in their physical features. And, sooner or later, when someone made commemts about their physical features, or treated them differently, they were shocked into recognition that they still had their Asian features and that others viewed them as Asian, not necessarily as a full-fledged American.

In grade school and, to a lesser degree, in secondary school, all adoptees, without exception, had experienced racial harassment from their peers. And, during adolescent years, most of them began to think about their birthmother, as they strived to integrate their dual heritages. For some, their desire to search for their birthmother was more intense than others. In high school, some experienced a sense of isolation from their white peers, owing to their being "different."

In college, some of the adoptees came in close contact with other Asian-American students, those who were adopted or of immigrant families, and found genuine comfort in their company and felt a sense of pride in themselves. Further, this feeling was translated into an appreciation of their Asian features—be it their black hair or dark eyes. For some, when they found a significant relationship with an Asian-American, that contact became a pivotal point for them to search for their birthmother or to become more interested in their country of origin. Such an experience tends to be more common among those who didn't bond well with their adoptive parents or those who were impacted by their newfound racial/ethnic awareness.

All adoptees acknowledged both benefits and losses, as a result of their adoption. Most of them felt a sense of loss for their birth family and struggled with some inner conflicts, dealing with racial or ethnic issues, but also felt they gained enormous benefits from being adopted and living in the United States.

One aspect I was particularly interested in learning from this research was: what factors most affect one's self-esteem? I started out with a set of assumptions that certain factors affect one's self-esteem more than others and that those factors are a loving and supportive relationship with parents or significant others, achievements by one's own efforts, one's belief system, coming to terms with one's racial/ethnic issues, and self-actualization.

All the factors listed above prove to be important

building blocks for the adoptees' self-esteem, but parental love and support seem to contribute foremost in building one's self-esteem. As attested in a few adoptees' cases in this research, the lack of parental love and support in their formative years often haunts throughout their young adult life. Some who had a turbulent relationship with their parents in adolescent years are still trying to rebuild their relationship with their parents. No matter how successful one may have been in academics or arts or sports, or in resolving identity questions, the one thing one can't escape seems to be the need to have a loving supportive relationship with their parents.

On the other hand, one adoptee, who received much parental love and support and excelled in academics and sports, had grappled with racial issues in college, which later were mitigated by his association with Asian-Americans. In this connection, he also found an avenue in which he could channel his talents and cross-cultural resources. This young adult asserts: "You look at your talents and resources, and try to make things happen for you." Indeed. The love and support he received from his parents may have given him a stable foundation, but what he does with what he has— self-actualization—is what really matters in the end.

While growing up, some adoptees in this study didn't have loving and supportive parents or struggled with inner conflicts. But it seems they all have made the most of themselves in their circumstances, in terms of where they came from. In the end, whatever they lacked or struggled

13

with seemed to have become their primary concern, which in turn served as a driving force in their lives. Moreover, out of their deeply felt experiences emerged valuable insights and convictions. And their views will certainly guide them in the course of time.

As you read their adoption experiences in this book, you will see they are an impressive group of adoptees, who are articulate, intelligent, insightful, and single-minded in pursuit of their goals. Some have been members of the National Honor Society or received various kinds of awards. Each of their stories has an organic unity which helps us to learn and understand their concerns, as well as the way they think and feel.

If material contained in this book renders new or additional insights in better understanding the issues facing the adoptees, and contributes to knowledge of intercountry adoption, the purpose of writing this book is fulfilled.

MATTHEW

(Age 18, Adopted at Age 7)

In Korea, I grew up on a farm, close to a big city, and lived with my parents, an elder sister, and two younger brothers. My father was a rice farmer; we had a TV, and probably our most prized possession was our ox. One day when I was six, my mother left for shopping in the city and told me to stay home, but I followed behind her in some distance, walking along the country road into the city. Once in the city, I lost my way back to my home in our village. The next thing I knew, I was picked up by the police who took me to the police station and then to an orphanage, where I stayed for a year* before coming to the States.

When I was seven, I came to the States to be adopted. I think I understood what adoption meant and what was

---

*Those children, who wandered in the street and were picked up by the police, usually stay in an orphanage for one year, during which time if no one claims them, they are assumed abandoned. Then the orphanage proceeds to place them for adoption.

going on. From the very beginning, my family had made a great deal of effort to make me feel at home. At first I wasn't comfortable with my Asian features or being different from my parents, but it was mostly in the first two months. I've always felt comfortable with my Asian features and I don't think about that any more. If other people feel uncomfortable with my features, that's their problem.

I'm glad I was adopted by my parents because they love me and care about me. I feel secure with them. Also, I'm glad because I have a chance at my dreams in the United States, which might not have been possible if I had stayed and lived in Korea.

When I was about ten, I began to remember what had happened to me in Korea. Also, I began to understand the meaning of my position and loss. Then when I was about twelve or thirteen years old, I began to feel bad and started to think about my birthparents. When I was about fifteen, I told my mom that I was lost from my birthmother. For a while, I had an intense desire to see my birthparents, but I got over that in the course of time. Yet I still remember and can see my birthmother's face and my birthfather working on the farm. Someday I would like to go and tell them I'm okay, and that I've never forgotten them.

In grade school, children in the first grade teased me about my Asian features. I realize now that they probably didn't know what they were doing. My reaction has always been that they are teasing me, not because they hate me, but they just don't understand me or know me. I'm not saying I

16

don't stand up to defend myself, but I'm not a violent person. Usually, I turn the other cheek.

In my studies, I like a little of everything. I like the challenge of school work and the physical and mental aspect of sports. I also like most kinds of artwork. Science is probably my favorite subject. English is probably the hardest subject for me. I make A's in all my subjects, maintaining a 3.80 g.p.a. Also, I've received various awards.

Right now I have many friends whom I met in school. They are all Caucasian of a middle-class background. They are all close to me. The only difference I have from them is that I have slanted eyes. It doesn't seem to make much difference to my friends. I think they've forgotten that I'm racially different from them. Some people told me, "You don't look Asian," and most of the time I don't feel like I'm Asian. I have no friends with Korean or any other Asian background. I don't intentionally go and seek them out.

I consider myself as American, because my home is in the United States where I have my American family and American friends, and I do American things. I love this country. Also, I'm proud of being Korean, but I don't value ethnic pride as much as other people do. Ethnic pride does not matter to me that much in functioning my daily life. For me, what matters more is having positive outlooks and a belief in a loving God.

My parents have always encouraged me to learn about Korea, but they have never pushed me. Right now I don't want to learn any more about Korea, but maybe someday I'll be interested in learning more about Korea.

I believe I have high self-esteem. I have good feelings about myself and have achieved success in my life. Others also say I have high self-esteem. The person who has helped me most is my mother. She has been with me everyday since I was adopted. She is always explaining, teaching, and guiding me in the right direction. Whatever I've achieved so far is also due to the fact that I've never looked back on my loss and have always strived to be the best person I can possibly be.

My immediate goal is to attend college. I'm accepted by a private university and plan to study premed. I hope to become a doctor of medicine someday.

SANDY

(Age 14, Adopted at Age 4)

When I was four, I came to the States. In Korea, I lived in a little hut with my father and my older sister. What I remember is little bits and pieces. I'm not sure if what I remember really happened. It's like a dream. I remember seeing my birthmother once or twice, when she visited us. My father worked at a factory and my older sister went to secondary school. During the daytime I stayed home and played with a neighbor's kid. My sister took care of me when she came home from school, and my father, when he returned from work. One day I went with my father to his work place, and he gave me some money to get some candy in a store across the street from the factory. I got a popsicle, and when I went back I didn't know in which building my father worked. I wandered about the area trying to find my father. Then, as I remember, I was picked up by the police who took me to the police station and then to an orphanage, where I stayed for a year before coming to the States.

When I came to the States I didn't cry or talk or say anything. I guess I was scared, because I didn't know what was happening.

Right now, I often feel left out. Sometimes I feel I'm not meant to be here. I can't really talk about my feelings. My brother and sister who were born to my parents have a better relationship with my parents. I get along with them, but I'm glad to have my brother who was also adopted from Korea, because I'm not the only person adopted in the family. One time I wished I hadn't been adopted and wished I were back in Korea, but not now. I like being adopted by a Caucasian couple and living in America rather than in Korea. We are financially better off here than we would be in Korea.

I think about going back to Korea someday. Although I think it's pretty impossible, I want to look for my birthfather and my older sister, with whom I lived in Korea. On the other hand, I don't think about my birthmother who didn't live with us and whom I saw only a few times.

I went to kindergarten for a couple of months and then open school programs all the way to junior high. When I attended kindergarten and grade school, some boys teased me about my eyes as "Chinese eyes." When I told my mom about the teasing, she said, "He shouldn't have said that. It isn't nice to say such a thing." When I was teased first time, I came home and cried. After that, it didn't bother me too much. If anyone does the teasing now, I just ignore it, but not many people do that now.

20

My favorite subject is English, particularly writing. I am good at math, and my teacher makes a lot of comments about that. Also, I like to create things, such as making a doll. I enjoy playing tennis; in fact, I'm on our school team.

I have many friends, but only a few close friends—one of them I used to take ballet lessons with, and the others are from my classes. Most of my friends are Caucasian whom I've known for a long time and with whom I go to the same school. I once had a couple of friends who were adopted from Korea, but we hardly see each other now. I wish I could make friends with Asian persons, but I don't have a strong desire to make friends on the basis of a similar racial or ethnic background. I make friends with whom I can get along or someone who has qualities that I admire, such as a sense of humor. When I get together with my friends, we talk about school work, boys, movies, other people, teachers, among other things.

I consider myself as Korean-American because I look Korean, but I'm really American in many other ways. Most of my peers don't know I was born in Korea. Most of the time I don't think about my Korean background or being Korean. At times I realize there are many differences between me and my friends. When people would look at me differently or stare at me, they make me feel like an odd ball. I hate my dark hair and my eyes. I wish sometimes I had different features, like having blond hair, because I guess I like to look like my friends or most of the others. My friends think I'm crazy because I wish I looked like them.

They say they like my dark hair and my complexion, but I don't like them.

For about three years, I belonged to the teen group at an adoption agency. My mom sent me there as she wanted me to learn something about Korea. The lady there cooked Korean meals, and that was the first time we ate real Korean food. My brother and I like Korean food, but I don't know very much about Korean culture or history. Later, I will learn about them. At the meeting we saw films which showed Korea, the people, and their customs. A lot of people dropped out of the group, including my friend, so I dropped out, too. I'm not interested in going there now. Also, it kind of got in the way of things I wanted to do.

I think I have an average self-esteem. I don't really have a big ego. But I'm a good student; I work hard to get good grades. Sometimes I'm really proud of myself for a piece of work I did.

FRANK

(Age 14, Adopted at Age 4)

When I was four years old, I came to the States to be adopted. In Korea, I lived in an orphanage with a bunch of girls and boys. All of us slept on the floor. I remember those days just being really poor. Before living in the orphanage, I lived with my father, stepmother, and a brother. My father worked at a shipyard, moving coals and doing heavy labor. I don't remember anything about my birthmother; she probably died. One day I got lost in the streets of my hometown and ended up in the orphanage. When I was living in the orphanage, I was told that someone in America wanted to adopt me. But I didn't really know a lot of things or what was really going on.

Since coming to the States, I have accepted my parents because they are the ones who wanted me and put in some money to adopt me. My parents are pretty open about adoption and freely talk about it with me and my sister, who was also adopted from Korea. When we were younger, we celebrated the anniversary of our arrival as a special day in our family.

On occasion, when I fight with my parents I say to them, "You give me a hard time because I'm adopted." But that's not true. You say these things because you are angry. In my case, it was great to be adopted. In fact, I like being adopted and living in America. However, being adopted can be embarrassing at times, especially when I introduce my friends to my parents. My friends get some ideas and ask me if I'm adopted or if my birthparents are Asian.

In general, I kind of like my life the way it is now. None of my friends give me any kind of hard time. If I were living in Korea with my birthparents, my life wouldn't be anything like this now. I won't be able to afford things I want to have. I like it here.

Sometimes I think about my birthfather and brother. Someday I would like to visit Korea and want to look for them. If they see me, I wonder what they would think of me or what I would think of them. If they wanted to get me back, that will be really sad.

All my life, I've gone to open school programs where most students came from minority groups. And I haven't encountered much racial teasing or prejudice.

The junior high I've just completed was so simple. We had only four classes, not a lot of academic study. It was kind of going over the same thing year after year. I was getting A's, but I think high school is going to be different. I like English—especially writing, but don't like reading. I'm not the kind of person who takes out books from the library to read. I like studio art, like drawing and painting, but hate to fire pottery. I'm interested in sports, such as soccer, tennis, and skiing.

Friends I have now are those I've met in the last three years. They are a lot more meaningful. My friends are mostly Caucasian, a few blacks, and no Asian. I am different from them, but it doesn't matter. They are really open with me. We get to know each other pretty well on one-to-one basis. They don't pick on me for being Korean or whatever. Occasionally, my friends joke about the way Asians speak English. If they make fun of me, they'll say, "I'm sorry." I have one close friend with whom I have a lot in common. We both like to play together—such as hockey, soccer, tennis, and skiing. We also like the same style of clothes.

My Asian features do not bother me. I like my complexion the way it is. My friends admire my tan; they all want to have some of the tan. But I wish my hair were lighter in color and wavy. In the society where I am, everyone is Caucasian—so I wish I looked more like them, not to be standing out. Sometimes I wish I had a mixed background; I think people with a mixed background look pretty nice.

I'm neither proud nor not proud of my Korean heritage. I guess I'm neutral. I don't know a lot about Korea, except what's going on TV. I don't know the language or the name of the President. I'm sure I'll learn later about Korea, but right now I'm not interested, not because I'm from Korea. I'm not interested in the history of Russia or any other countries, either. American history isn't even too thrilling to me. I don't like social studies.

At one time, my parents sent me to the teen-group meetings at an adoption agency. One thing I learned there and remember is the traditional Korean wedding. It was pretty formal and boring. However, it was fun to get together with other teenagers of a similar background, but we didn't have much in common. Also, we didn't get the chance to know each other. I'm not going to their meetings any more and I've quit now.

My self-esteem ranges from low to high, depending on things. I guess my low self-esteem has to do with my tendency to change myself or do things to please others. If my friends say, "Your shoes are tacky," I won't wear those shoes. I guess what I really want is basically what others want—that is, just being "in" with the trend.

On the other hand, my self-esteem is pretty high in certain areas. I wouldn't do things, simply because my friends ask me to. It's got to be a pretty good reason, and not anything that would hurt me or other people. For example, if my friends ask me, "Take joint, it's cool." I wouldn't take it because I don't want to get into it. From the films I saw at school, I'm pretty well aware of the effects of taking drugs or alcohol. It's scary what it can do to you. Also, I have a definite preference for a certain style in clothes and stick to what I like. It's one of the things that builds up my self-esteem.

For a career, I plan to go to a vocational college and take classes in home economics, such as cooking, interior decoration, designing clothes or clothes merchandising.

CHRIS

(Age 16, Adopted at Age 1½)

The adoption agency told us that I was abandoned as an infant on the door step of an orphanage. When I was one and a half years old, I came to the States to be adopted.

From early ages on, my mom read me books on adoption, which explained why a child is adopted. So I've always known that I was adopted. I've also felt comfortable with my Asian features, and have never felt uncomfortable being different from my parents. I feel I'm unique. If I were Caucasian like my parents, I guess I'd lose some of my uniqueness.

I have great parents. They love me and I love them. I feel secure with them because they've always been supportive of me in the past and hope they will be supportive in the future, too.

Sometimes I think about my birthparents when I come home, particularly after a bad day in school. I've often thought about them, wondering why they gave me up for adoption. Was it because they didn't want me or because they thought it the best for me. I wish I had known my birthmother. I have a lot of questions I would like to ask her. Someday I would like to visit Korea and find her.

When I was younger and attended an all-white school, kids used to make fun of me, but as they got older they stopped doing that. When I first moved here to the South, people were so mean. They used to call me all sorts of names, like "flat face" or "Chinese," which I hated. I used to cry a lot because of this. They also mimicked stereotype Asian gestures or speech. When I discussed the incidents with my mom, she told me that it was the name-caller who had a problem, and that there was nothing wrong with me. She also advised me to ignore the person, if possible; if that didn't work, she suggested that I stand up for myself by telling them to "get lost" or "blow it out your ear." The people I run into now don't care about my Asian features. Appearance isn't a major issue any more.

My academic interests are history, business, and education. I have no artistic ability, but I love music. My average grade is B+. I like all subjects, but hate grammar and writing. I love to read, but hate to analyze and critique.

I have many casual friends and a few close friends, whom I met at school or at parties. They don't care about my being Asian; they like me the way I am as a person. My friends are mostly Caucasian with a few blacks and Indians. I don't associate with people on the basis of nationality or ethnic heritage.

I consider myself as Korean-American, because the United States is my home country and Korea is my birth country. I'm neither proud nor not proud of being Korean-born. I think too much pride hinders rather than helps. I'm interested in learning about Korea someday, as I am about any other countries. Right now, I have more important things to do.

I feel comfortable with my Asian features, although at one time I felt uncomfortable. When I was in the sixth grade, my hair bothered me most, but now this doesn't bother me. I think being Asian is lucky in the United States; I've never faced a situation in which I felt I couldn't do things because of my race.

I have high self-esteem. I like myself; I like the way I am, even though I may not please everybody.

MARTHA

(Age 20, Adopted at Age ½)

According to the adoption agency, I was left on the door step of an orphanage. Then I was placed in foster care for a month, before I was brought over here to be adopted. I was six months old.

My parents wanted a child, but couldn't conceive, so they adopted me from Korea. At the time, that was considered as the easiest and fastest way. They were so happy with their adoption of me that they planned to adopt another child from Korea. Two years after they adopted me, my mom gave birth to a boy, my brother, to whom I am very close.

When I was little, my mom often read to me an adoption story from a book that told why a child is adopted. So I grew up knowing that I was adopted from Korea. I was basically accepted by my mom's relatives, but dad's mom was very much against adopting a Korean child. Although she had problems in the beginning, she has learned to accept me over the years.

In my teen years, I had some conflict with my dad about using his car. He didn't want me to use it and drive a long distance. We often fought about that. Also, my dad objected to my going out with my cousin. That was upsetting at the time. When I didn't keep their curfew, I was grounded for two weeks.

During my high school years, my dad helped me a great deal with school work, especially with calculus. My parents were very supportive of me on whichever career I wanted to enter. When I said I wanted to be a nurse they thought that was great. For a while, my mom wanted me to go into dancing. I used to do many kinds of dancing—such as slow dance, tap, or ballet. Since one doesn't earn a lot of money from dancing, I decided not to continue with it as a career.

I'm very secure in my relationship with my parents. When I'm faced with a hard decision, I always go to my parents, because their opinions are very important to me. They give their opinion but say, "You have to do what you think best for you and face the consequences." I'm decisive and willing to make a decision and go with that.

I feel very fortunate because my parents have been great. I feel they raised me very well and gave me a lot of love and support. And I'm glad I grew up in America. I wouldn't change that for anything. If I were adopted by a Korean family and grew up in Korea, I would probably feel fortunate too, but there is no way for me to know that.

Certainly, my circumstances would have been different if I had stayed in Korea. I wouldn't have the nice life that I have now.

As I get older, I wonder about my birthmother, but I don't have a particular desire to seek her out. I believe that she made the best decision for me by leaving me near the orphanage. My mom also said, "What your birthmother did was the best decision she made for you—to have a better life." When my parents asked me if I wanted to meet my birthparents, I said I had no desire to seek them out. My only desire is to obtain my medical background.

In elementary school, I ran into some teasings about my eyes from older kids who didn't know me, but never from my classmates. They made me mad, but I never cried. I just ignored them. I was very young then, and confronting them wouldn't have done much good on my behalf. I never told my mom about the teasing incidents because I thought she couldn't have done very much either.

In high school, I was in the honors class. In my freshman year at the University, I achieved straight A's one quarter. In the University's business school I'm now attending, my grades are not as high, because everybody is on the same level and pursuing more or less the same major, and competition is very high. I'm highly motivated in my studies, because I want to find a good job that would afford me a lifestyle that I want to live, including traveling and a lot of entertainment.

I've always been outgoing, so I make friends easily.

From high school on, all my close friends have been Caucasian, and I have never wanted to replace good friends. In high school, I was a cheerleader and was in the popular crowd, which included a homecoming queen. Although I faced some pressure with drinking, I decided not to drink too much.

In high school, I didn't date a lot, but dated only Caucasian boys and one biracial boy. I'm comfortable dating Caucasians with whom I grew up. I haven't yet met or dated any Asian-Americans. Basically, I'd be interested in dating anyone who is interesting, regardless of ethnic background. If I lived in California, I would probably have more chances to date Asian-Americans. My parents don't have any preference as to my date's ethnic background, as long as he is a nice guy. Recently, I met a Caucasian guy; there was attraction for both of us, but we never went out on a date. He said, "My grandparents would never go for that." I thought that was dumb, because I considered him better than that.

I consider myself as Korean-American because I was born in Korea and look Korean, but I feel American. I think that all my personality traits and attitudes are American, as well as my gestures and views.

When I was growing up in the white suburbs, naturally I wanted to be American, and I didn't think much about my ethnic background. When I was in the fourth grade, I wished I had blond hair as my best girlfriend had blond hair. Now I'm glad the way I am. I like my black hair.

Now you have to pay me to have blond hair.

Although my parents never asked me if I wanted to learn about Korean culture, once my parents brought me a couple of books on Korea to look at. Also, whenever Korea was on the news, my dad always tried to get my attention so that I might learn about it. I'm sure if my parents knew about a place that taught Korean culture and if I wanted to learn about it, they would probably have sent me there. They wanted me to do things pretty much as I wanted to do.

As I grow older, I'm getting more interested in Korean culture, particularly their current life style. Korean history isn't a big issue with me right now. My Korean friend at work, who immigrated with her parents, tells me about Korean customs that I find are so very different from American customs. I also learn from her that there are a lot of racists in Korea, as well as here in the States. It seems that racism exists everywhere and in all countries.

I have high to average self-esteem and feel good about myself. I think that self-esteem depends on how you were raised by your parents. If your parents loved you and encouraged you to do things that are good for you and that you wanted to do, you're going to have high self-esteem and confidence in dealing with things in your life. From the age of six months to twenty years, I haven't had any tragedies or traumas in life, nor have I had to deal with huge issues in life or with my inner self. I've had a good life.

I think it's important for one to have high self-esteem.

People want to be with those who have high self-esteem, individuality, and good feelings about themselves. People don't have patience with those who put themselves down constantly, because you get tired of complimenting them everyday or every hour on the hour.

I don't think your sense of racial/ethnic identity has anything to do with your self-esteem. However, I think that for those kids who didn't get a lot of love and support from their parents, their knowledge about their ethnic heritage would help build their self-esteem.

My immediate goal after graduating from college is to find a job that I like doing. From there, other dreams and goals will follow.

BRIAN

(Age 21, Adopted at Age 4)

According to the agency report, I was supposedly abandoned at a marketplace. But what I remember is this: when I was about three and a half, my father died. Then I remember going to my father's funeral and that he was cremated. Sometime after that, my mother remarried. In view of conventional Korean customs* and financial circumstances, my birthmother apparently decided to place me for adoption and my sister with a relative. I vaguely remember saying "goodbye" to my sister when she left. Then I distinctly remember going with my mother to a building in my hometown, which was probably an agency of some sort. I remember being left in a room before I was

---

*Traditionally, in Korea, when a woman gets divorced from her husband, she leaves her children in the custody of her husband. If her husband dies and she remarries, she usually places her children with the relatives of her deceased husband, as the mother doesn't have much claim to her children. Also, her new husband is often unwilling to assume the responsibility for raising her children by her previous husband. In such a situation, the mother hasn't much choice, but give her children away to relatives or, as in recent years, resort to place them for adoption, preferably by American couples.

sent to Seoul, where I was placed in a foster home in the rural area near Seoul. We lived in a traditional Korean house, and I remember riding a goat on the farm. In the second foster home, there were two children, one an infant and the other older than me. I was given a lot of housework to do, like going to the open-air market to get coal briquettes or taking care of the infant. They didn't feed me well, and I was always hungry.

Before coming to the States, I remember getting shots at a medical facility near Namdaemun in Seoul. And just before departing for the States, the agency gave me a set of clothes—a blue shirt with "U.S.A." on it and a toy (red cement truck). The flight to the States was fine.

When I got off the plane in the United States, I was so scared that I wished I were back in Korea. Coming out of the plane to meet my new family was a traumatic experience. My adoptive family and all the relatives were there. I was terrified, looking at their strange faces and seeing their arms flying at me. When they picked me up, I cried and thrashed my arms at them. When my sister gave me a stuffed animal, I threw it at her. A tall Korean man came over to me and said in Korean, "That's your adoptive parents," and pushed me along toward them.

After the initial shock, I continued to have nightmares for a month, screaming in Korean. My parents were uptight, not knowing what to do with me. The agency suggested that they record me while I was screaming, and play that back to me. When I heard myself speaking in Korean from the tape, I was shocked and confused, because I didn't understand how I was speaking to myself. Before that, all I had been hearing was English. After that shock, I stopped my nightmares. The content of my nightmares, which I found out later, was that I was cursing my birthmother for relinquishing me and putting me where I was. So I had a lot of anger toward her at the time. It was a gradual transition in which I worked out my grief and frustration, and adjusted to a new culture, as well as accepted being adopted.

My parents had a daughter who was born to them. They adopted me because they couldn't have another child and wanted a son. From the beginning, I knew that I was different from the rest of my family, and that they were not my birthparents. My parents were open about adoption and they read me a book on adoption, which explained why a child is adopted. They asked me if I thought about my birthmother and inquired about my experience in Korea. At that age, I couldn't remember specific things that had happened to me in the past. Also, due to the lack of my English facility, I was unable to get my memories together and articulate them.

Growing up in my Caucasian family in the suburbs had become quite normal to me. But, from early ages on, I realized that I was "different" and not the norm. In fact, people kept telling me that I was adopted. And as I didn't have pictures of myself as a baby, I was always conscious of being adopted. On occasion, I felt a little uneasy or embarrassed—especially in grade school when there was an open house each fall and parents were invited to meet the new teacher. The teachers were invariably surprised when they met my parents, as they were expecting my parents to be Asian. When my parents introduced themselves as "Brian's parents," the teacher smiled and acknowledged the fact by saying, "Oh, I see." On the other hand, having white parents made it easier for me to adapt to American culture than I would have with Korean parents.

When I was growing up, my parents worked full-time and provided well for me and my sister. We took family vacations to different parts of the country, such as Florida, and to Caribbean Islands one winter. At the same time they gave us a lot of housework to do at a young age, such as preparing dinners, doing dishes, and the yardwork. When I looked at my friends, they didn't seem to have as much housework to do as I had to do and at the time, I had a certain amount of resentment. But now looking back, I'm glad they gave me the responsibility, because that helped me to grow up quicker than other kids of my age. All my relatives accepted me. I'm particularly close to my grandparents, and aunts to some extent.

My parents had high expectations from us in our academic performance and social conduct. They were supportive when I played in various kinds of school sports, and came to see me when I played in the games. During my high school years, I changed my occupational goals many times. They didn't really pressure me to choose any particular occupation, but allowed me to decide on my own. However, they stressed the value that doing things one wants to do is more important than making a lot of money. When I got to college I really enjoyed art and decided to concentrate on it. They never discouraged me by saying, "If you become an artist you'll starve," but supported me in my decision.

Up to high school, I was more of an introvert, seemingly passive, and held a lot of anger inside. I didn't confide my problems in others and tried to deal with them by myself, because I had a certain sense of pride and self-reliance. I tended to be alone and felt comfortable being alone. This created social barriers with friends. I related to people on a social level, but if my relationship moved to a personal level, I tended to go back to the social level.

In my teen years, I had some conflicts with my parents, mainly due to my desire to be independent. A lot of conflicts arose when they tried to suggest or interfere with what I was doing. They tried to help me, but the way I was at the time I didn't want any help and simply wanted to be left alone. You develop an attitude that you think you know more than they do and decide they don't understand you. So you figure you can't relate to them. And you get into arguments on anything and everything.

Right now, I'm pretty secure in my relationship with my parents. We keep in close contact. I talk to them once or twice every week and see them every two weeks. In general, I feel very fortunate being adopted—particularly by my parents. When I compare my experience with that of other adoptees, many are not as fortunate as I am. They seem to have a lot of conflicts with their parents. Not only domestic conflicts, but also they have had negative experiences in their community, particularly those in the rural areas, where there is much ignorance and intolerance.

Living in the States has provided me a lot of opportunity for a better life, in terms of economic, educational, psychological, and spiritual well-being, than I would have had in Korea. And I have a high level of international awareness that allows me to have a broader point of view on what's happening in other countries. If I lived in Korea, I wouldn't have that level of awareness, as Korea is preoccupied with its own economical, social, and cultural concerns, much less with what's going on in the rest of the world. Growing up in America, I'm, of course, biased in Euro-American values. And I'm pretty open-minded and liberal, and have a high tolerance level for people who are different from the norm. If I had grown up in Korea, I wouldn't have that tolerance and openness. But I can't know what I don't know.

On the other hand, as a result of my adoption, I feel a sense of loss for my birth family and my birth culture. When I think of my birthparents, I feel a sense of sadness. I do fantasize about them. The thoughts of my birthmother has been constant with me ever since I came to the States. When I was in grade school, my parents used to send me up to my room as punishment; I would think then of my birthmother and would get angry at her for putting me where I was. Also, I wished she were there with me, then I would cry.

Gradually, as I began to understand why she gave me up, negative feelings toward her had turned to positive feelings. I began to hold a certain amount of respect toward her, and I often thought about her. Still, I recognized all along there was a hole in me, but I didn't know how to fill it. When I was a high school junior, my parents asked me if I wanted to go to Korea for a trip and offered to help me with the trip, but I didn't want to, because I wasn't ready for it or mature enough. Then, during my freshman year in college, I felt a tremendous urge to fill the hole in me. Recently, I took a trip to Korea in the hope of finding my birthmother, and also to fill my emotional needs. Before leaving for Korea, I wrote my parents a note in which I explained the purpose of my trip and stated that I considered them as my real parents and had no intention of renouncing them.

On the trip I didn't find my birthmother, due to lack of sufficient information, but in the next two years or so, I'm definitely going back to Korea to find her. While in Korea, I found myself very comfortable living among the people of my nationality, even though a lot of them were negative about adopted people. The important thing was that I felt less pressure in everyday life, because I didn't have to deal with racial issues.

Also, I have some inner conflicts because I was forced

into circumstances where I had no control and had to adapt to them. The one thing I want adoptive parents to know is that most of us adoptees didn't have a choice when we came to the States to be adopted. We didn't ask to leave our country or to leave our birthmother. By circumstances, we were essentially forced to leave them. At times we may feel sorry for ourselves, but we don't expect anyone to adopt us as a favor or out of social obligations by thinking, "We are so fortunate. Let's help someone who is in need of a home." I think that a lot of couples adopted us, precisely for that reason, with no commitment to love us as their child. To those couples I'd like to say, "Don't adopt." I know some of the adoptees have been disowned by their adoptive parents. And I suspect that is a result of their being insincere about their motivations at the time of adoption.

The schools I attended from grade to high were largely made up of Caucasian students, with some Southeastern Asians. In grade school, I was teased a lot because children didn't understand why I looked different from them. Often, they called me names, like "chink" or "Jap," by pulling the ends of their eyes up with their index fingers. I ignored as much as I could and gave them a chance to stop, but they persisted. On occasion, if I confronted them, they would come back with others. At times I got into fights, but didn't tell my parents, because I felt ashamed. On one occasion, when I got into a fight, the offender and I were called into the principal's office. I told the principal that the guy called me names, but I didn't say specifically what kind of names he called. He said, "That's no reason to fight. You shouldn't fight." We were thus reprimanded, but he chose to ignore the fact that the other person instigated the fight.

In high school, my ability in sports gave me confidence. My peers accepted me readily into their circle, because of my athletic ability. Once in their circle, I often heard them talking about other Asians and making fun of the way they spoke English. That made me feel uncomfortable. But they would say, "Brian, we're not making fun of you—you are like us." Nevertheless, I felt uncomfortable because what they were doing was wrong. I said, "I look like them and associate with them. When you tease them, you are teasing me, also." I felt they put me as a target for the other Asians, whom they were mimicking. At first, I ignored their teasing, but when they persisted, I chose to dissociate from them.

Also, my peers accepted me readily, because I had Caucasian parents rather than Asian parents. In a way, having Caucasian parents served me well, to my advantage. I know some parents of my peers, who are blatantly racist, accepted me because I had Caucasian parents. They had a lot of communication with my parents, and to them, I was in a vague territory and they didn't know what to do with me. I'm sure they had negative feelings about me being Asian, but didn't show because my parents were Caucasian like themselves.

From grade to high school, I was a good student, among the top five percent of my class. In high school, I was initiated into the National Honor Society. Math,

English, and art were my favorite subjects, in all of which I did well. I also excelled in sports and received various kinds of awards. Recently I won a design competition, and my model for stone work was selected for public construction.

The main source of my motivation is my grandfather whom I respect a lot. I respect him for his integrity and character. My grandparents are also very generous with me and my sister. They are my role models. Another source is my Japanese-American professor at college, who is influential in my work. He is Asian-American, to whom I can relate about his coming over from Japan and his experience in the States.

Friends I had in high school were quite different from those I have now. From grade through high school, most of my friends were Caucasian and a few acquaintances of Asian-Americans. During those years I chose to be associated with Caucasians, because it was easier for me to make friends with them than with Asians. Also, at the time I had negative views of Asians. I often found myself trying to be someone that I was not—in order to please other people, and I developed low self-esteem. I didn't have confidence in myself. At the same time I tended to drop back from a lot of social groups that consisted of Caucasians, and experienced a sense of isolation.

Now, my choice of friends is more diverse. While most of my friends are Asians, I also have friends who are Caucasian, black, and Hispanic. This is a result of my education, changes in my attitude, my recognition of my racial identity, and my desire to deal with that identity.

In high school, I used to date Caucasian girls, consciously or unconsciously, because they were considered more desirable, in terms of social power vested in their race, and also they were more available where I was. Now, since I started college, I date Asian-Americans whom I meet at the social or educational activities that involve Asian-Americans. In the recent past, I dated Asian-Americans—one from East Asia and two from Southeast Asia.

At this time, I identify myself as Asian-American. When I was young, my parents sent me to Korean culture camp which was held at a church. They dealt with superficial aspects of Korean culture, such as food, clothes, Taekwondo, fan dance, and the like. They treated Korean culture as a novelty and looked at it merely as an exotic foreign culture.

Now looking back, I wish that my parents had encouraged me more to learn about Korean culture, when I was growing up. In a way they did, but at the time I wasn't interested. It was my fault. I wish that they had lived in a different city environment, where there were more minorities. The suburbs where I grew up was a great place to grow up, but I had no role models who looked like me. So I thought I looked Caucasian, but I was not ready to accept that, because I knew I looked different. I know that a lot of Korean adoptees do not view themselves as a minority, and they forget the fact that they are Asian, probably in their desire to be part of the white culture.

Also, they are not conscious of the fact that others (non-Asians) view them as a minority, in terms of their looks and their ethnic origin. And they get shocked or amazed when others view them as a minority and treat them differently. I think it's serious and funny that they are oblivious to the fact that society views them as Asians. Their lack of awareness is probably due to the fact that they were so conditioned by their parents, the white culture, and social pressures.

In college, which was in a small Midwestern town, I encountered my racial awakening. The racial prejudice I encountered there was worse than I ever experienced in grade school. The school's atmosphere was very tense. When you walked around the campus, white students would give you unfriendly glances. There was a lot of verbalization of racism by white students toward minority students, especially against blacks by referring to them as "niggers." Maybe they thought I wouldn't be offended by that, since I was Asian, but I was offended. Also, people in the town were filled with racial paranoia. When my roommate and I walked down the streets, some people, who had negative feelings about the Vietnamese War, called out at us with a racial epithet and insult, like "Go home!" Racial paranoia seemed stronger and more pervasive because it was a small town. When you live in a big city, racial prejudice tends to be diffused.

To deal with racial paranoia, I went through regular channels of the student government and college president, and tried to handle the problem in a responsible way, but their attitudes were very negative. What they told me basically was, "If you don't like it here, go somewhere else." So I did, along with other Asian students. It was a big growing-up year for me. As I recognized that there was racial hatred and bias in the society, I began to question, "Who am I?" and did research on my own to deal with my racial identity and social conditions in the United States.

My parents understand my need to be with other Asians and actually encouraged me to participate in an Asian community. And being involved in the Asian community, I'm trying to find my racial identity. But my parents don't understand my experience with my peers or I can't fully share my experience with them. As a result, I feel a bit isolated from them; yet I don't have conflicts or uneasy feelings because of that. The task I'm facing now is to adapt myself to my environment and accept my roles in different situations. In my parents' house, I act differently from that when I'm in an Asian person's house. Even my thought process becomes different in each situation.

Since my association with Asian-Americans, I've developed a solid foundation of my racial identity. When I have a firm grasp of my racial identity I feel more confident. I think it is important to have a strong identification with Asian culture, but the more important thing is what aspect of the culture one identifies with. I know that I can't identify with certain aspects of Asian culture, probably because of some of the values I was brought up with in the

United States.

On the other hand, my self-identity is defined through my art work, a product of my creative expression, which affects everything I do—how I think and to whom I relate. By expressing my thoughts or ideas artistically, I define my self-identity and values I deal with. My racial identity being part of my self-identity, a lot of racial issues also come through my art work. And I learn from my art work about my identity; others also learn from it about my identity. I feel I have high self-esteem, as a result of positive reinforcements that I receive from my parents, my peers, and others for what I do.

My immediate goal is to find my birthmother and complete a degree in my field. I may study further to get an advanced degree. Right now, I teach photography to Asian-American students, as a medium for reaching higher goals. Ultimately, I want to do something useful for society or to benefit others in some small ways by using my art work.

ANNE

(Age 22, Adopted at Age 2½)

After my father died due to an illness, my birthmother couldn't support all of us four children. So she decided to relinquish my brother and me, the younger of the children, for adoption, and placed us in the care of an orphanage. I came to the States, when I was two and a half years old.

My adoptive mother had a health problem and didn't want to have children. Her problem is now under control, and she is very healthy and active. When my parents decided to adopt a child, the agency offered them two siblings who needed to be placed together.

When we were old enough to recognize the differences between us and my parents, they told that we were adopted from Korea. And they explained that my birthmother relinquished the two of us for adoption, because she had no means to take care of us, but she wanted us to have a better life.

When I was young, my mom carried me on her back.

She took a cooking class at Korean school so she could prepare some Korean food. We often had rice and kimchi as part of our meals. At one point my parents sent us to Korean school, but we didn't like it. When we were young, we celebrated the anniversary of our arrival, remembering what we did that day—arriving at the airport, meeting our parents, and coming to our home.

Since we were the first adopted children on both sides of my parents, we were a big adjustment to the family. But my relatives accepted us as we were, not because of where we came from. We are closer to our relatives on my mother's side. Particularly my maternal grandparents accepted us with love and caring. One of our relatives is adopting a girl from Korea because they enjoy having us.

While growing up, my parents provided us well with things that we needed or wanted—although we earned some of the things we got by doing our housework. I feel very happy being adopted and living in America. I don't think I could have a better life. My parents are wonderful and very understanding. When I had questions about my background, they tried to answer as much and openly as they could. I feel very close to my parents and feel fortunate that they adopted my brother and me—to love us as their children. They gave us love and understanding that we needed. We think we are lucky in that, because I know some adoptees didn't get that from their parents.

Also my parents have been very helpful in other areas, as well. Mom helped with my term papers by correcting mistakes and my dad by providing me with reference books that I needed to do homework. Math, science, and language have been difficult subjects for me—and my parents have always encouraged me to do well on these subjects. When I decided to take a break from college, they supported my decision by saying that it's better to be happy than unhappy. My parents taught me values—to be kind and not pass judgments quickly of others. I always think people are good when I meet and learn if they are not. They also taught me to share with others and be generous.

Out in public, I've never felt uncomfortable being with my Caucasian parents, because I consider us as my family. At the same time, I never wished I looked like Caucasian. Even if you wished that, you can't change that. I'm proud of who I am and how I look. Nobody should feel ashamed of that. Although acquaintances who hadn't met my parents assumed that my parents were also Asian, I usually tell my friends that I was adopted; so they never asked me further questions. Here in the Midwest, multiracial families—particularly those of Asian children with Caucasian parents—are not unusual. Strangers never treated us unkindly, although they gave us a second glance. In Korea, to which we took a trip when I was a teenager, we got many more glances and comments from strangers than we did here. It was obvious to them that we were a multiracial family of Caucasian parents and Asian children. They probably guessed that we were adopted from Korea.

Although I feel comfortable being adoped, I also feel a

sense of loss for my birth family and my birth culture. But if I stayed in the orphanage, knowing the conditions I was in and knowing the kind of life I might have led, I truly believe that I would have died of malnutrition. When I was adopted, I was considerably undernourished for my age. In the orphanage where I stayed, I guess I wasn't getting enough food. When I compare my gains and losses, I've gained ten times more than I've lost. In Korea, I don't think I could have lived a full life as I have here in the States.

As long as I can remember, I've always thought about my birthmother and sisters, wondering if they are leading a happy or unhappy life. I've never felt anger or bitterness toward my birthmother—because she did the best she could for my brother and me at the time, no doubt out of her desire for us to have happiness and a fuller life.

During my teen years, when I indicated my wish to find my birthmother, my parents supported me on that, and they wrote a letter to the orphanage where I had stayed before coming to the States. Then, when I was in my teen years, all of us in my family took a trip to Korea hoping to find my birthmother and sisters. We went to the orphanage where we stayed. They told us that my birthmother had written them inquiring if anyone from the adoptive family came and asked about her; she suggested that if anyone came, the orphanage could share any information they had. But they said no one from my birth family came back and asked about us. Anyway, we tried to locate my birthmother. Even though we didn't succeed in finding her, we were glad that we tried. We had a great trip and have no regrets. If we met our birthmother and sisters, it would have been a plus. I plan to go back when I'm older and look for my birthmother, hopefully she will be healthy and alive, and that she would tell me about my father.

The schools I went to over the years were predominantly populated by white students. While math, language, and science were hard subjects for me, I did well in art and athletic areas. I was an average student. One thing I'm proud of having done is that I was selected for the state-sponsored trip to Russia with a group of outstanding students, as a result of my application which included a brief essay and interview. I raised half of the money for the trip, with the help of my parents. The trip was a wonderful experience for me that I shall treasure for a long time.

In grade school, a few students teased me and called me a name, which was upsetting, but it wasn't worth making a big fuss about. As I advanced in schooling, there were more Asians or blacks in the student body. Nobody really teased or bothered me a whole lot because I was Asian and looked "different."

Peer pressure never was a problem, because I was independent by nature. I didn't belong to a clique, but I had a close girlfriend to whom I could relate. Now I have a variety of friends coming from different ethnic groups, whom I met in college, but the majority of them is Caucasian. My best friend is Caucasian, whom I met in the second grade and grew up together.

In high school, I didn't date that much, but dated mostly Caucasian guys with blond hair and blue eyes, and one Asian guy from Hawaii. I don't particularly prefer any ethnic group, but I've been brought up in an environment which was populated by Caucasians. I don't think I've ever been rejected because of my ethnic background. Maybe there were guys who didn't ask me out because of my being Asian, but I'm not aware of that. Those guys who are concerned about what their friends might say or think about my racial/ethnic origin are not worth my time or attention.

In college, I dated guys coming from a variety of racial backgrounds—Caucasian, black, but mostly Caucasian. I have never dated Asian men, not because I didn't want to, but I wasn't asked by them. The racial or ethnic background of my dates has never been a big issue to me. I don't think one should date someone simply because they look like me. I think what is more important is to date someone with whom one can get along. Although my parents didn't like some of the guys I dated, they didn't try to influence me one way or the other. All they wanted for me was to choose those whom I liked and felt comfortable with.

During my teen years, I had no serious conflicts with my parents, except that I wanted to be more independent than they expected me—like staying out later than they wanted me. However, I had an identity crisis of sorts and saw a therapist for a while. The therapist didn't understand what I was going through and couldn't support me the way

I needed. So I stopped going to see her. But she helped me, in terms of getting out some of the feelings I had. I dealt with my problems by talking to friends. Having someone you could relate to about what you were experiencing was most helpful to me. That was the kind of therapy I needed.

At the time, two things bothered me most and still do to some extent. One thing is having to do with the questions of ethnic identity. Some Americans don't see me as "being American," even though I was brought up as American on American values, and act and dress like Americans. They see us as Korean or Asian, but not as American, and they do not see us as their equal. Similarly, many of the immigrant Asian-Americans I run into in college do not identify with me. They see me as being different from them. Of all different nationalities, I feel particularly more uncomfortable toward immigrant Korean-Americans who don't identify with us adoptees, because we were adopted by Caucasian parents and brought up on American values. That's hard to take. I try to talk to them; they look at me differently and don't treat me as their equal. And that makes the adoptees feel stuck in the middle, not being accepted by either group as their equal. As a result, we adoptees experience a lot of confusion.

Another thing is that in the high school I attended, I experienced a lot of stares from refugee students from Southeast Asia. Whenever I walked down the halllways, they always stared at me and you could tell they were talking about me. They would ask teachers about me—

where I was from and what kind of background I had. That made me feel more uncomfortable than anything else. I could sense that they were resentful toward me. And also, when I go to a Chinese restaurant with friends, people would stare at me. I understand that people in different Asian countries can tell the differences between the different Asian nationalities. I don't understand why they stare at me. My friends see me, first and foremost, as a person and as their friend, not primarily as an ethnic entity.

WENDY

(Age 22, Adopted at Age 4½)

When I was four and a half years old and my younger brother two and a half, we came to the States to be adopted together by a Caucasian couple. I learned from my parents that my birthparents died and we were under our grandmother's care with an older sister.

I have always known that I was adopted and have felt comfortable being with my parents or being around Caucasian people. I feel very fortunate being adopted by a Caucasian family—maybe because that's all I know. Maybe my life would be different if I had been adopted by a Korean family.

After adopting us, my parents adopted another Korean girl, then two biracial girls, and then gave birth to two children. I'm very proud of our multiracial family. When people give us a second look, I hope they will stop and think about what it takes to become a multiracial family. For me, it's very natural to be in a multiracial family. I had a good childhood. My parents always wanted us to know that they loved us. It didn't matter if we were adopted or not. They treated us all equally. I've never felt that my parents were adoptive parents. When my friends ask me, "Are they your real parents?" I always feel and say, "They are my real parents." We never went through conflicts about issues surrounding adoption. Only once, when I was really angry, I said, "You're doing this to me because I'm adopted," to hurt their feelings. I didn't really mean that at all; afterward, I felt I wasn't being fair.

As a family, we did many things together that were related to interracial adoption, involving black or Asian children. I think that was a good learning experience for us. But we didn't have a chance to learn Korean culture and language or to interact with other Asian persons. When we were young, my parents encouraged us to go to Korean school, but we didn't appreciate going to Korean classes, because we didn't want to be Korean then, as we wanted to be American. One summer, when they sent us to the Korean culture camp, we found that many other children knew each other because they had been there before, but we didn't know anyone. So we felt a bit isolated from other children. Now, in retrospect, I wish my parents had sent us every year or at least every other year.

When I reached my teen years, I clashed a lot with my parents, which was probably not greatly different from any other families. If things could be done in two ways, my parents wanted to have their way. Being strong-headed myself, I wanted to do things my way. My parents were being too strict and always controlling. So when I was eighteen, I moved out from that environment. I wanted to have some control over my life and to grow as a person. It's been easier for me.

Right now, my parents and I are building our relationship. I talk with them once a week or two weeks. I feel secure in my relationship with them, knowing that they love me. Only I wish that they could have been more helpful financially, when I wanted to go to college. They said, "If you want to go to college you must pay your way. When I went to college I had to pay my way. You can do that, too." But I wish they could have been more supportive financially, knowing that they're actually investing in me by helping me to go to college. Maybe that's selfish on my part.

My parents did a lot of good for me. They are strong individuals who pursue what they believe in, regardless of what other people think or say. When they adopted us, my grandparents did not encourage them. So they had to really fight for us to be accepted into their family. My parents ultimately want us to be happy. My Dad said, "I don't care whatever you decide to do, but as long as you're happy, I'd be happy for you." He feels I have the potential to do more than what I'm doing now. I'd like to pursue a career in which I could use my artistic ability in drawing, but I know it wouldn't provide a good living.

Living in the United States, I have gained a lot. I speak English without a foreign accent. American people are more open-minded about interracial matters, and I've also learned to be open-minded. I hear that Korean men are domineering over the women, but here, men and women are more equal. That's a big gain.

At times I thought about my birthparents, but when I was young I was told that they were dead. I don't have a great deal of interest to visit Korea. Someday I'd like to go to Korea to find out what had actually happened to my parents, but I accept my parents here. I think I have an older sister and am curious about her. If I want to make a trip to Korea, my parents are all for it, but I have to provide for the trip myself.

Throughout my school years, I was an average student academically, but excelled in drawing and dance. I was the captain of dance line after my second year. In school activities, I was both included and excluded.

In elementary school, I felt comfortable being the only Asian among all white kids. Most of the students liked me, but a few boys acted mean toward me. In my teenage years, I had one or two close friends and many acquaintances whom I met at school. But, in general, I felt being isolated the way many others felt insecure about themselves. No one came out to say, "Wendy, I really like you." Particularly, in my senior year at high school, I felt isolated and spent a lot of time alone, reading or drawing.

Right now, I have a few close friends who are strong, dependable, and supportive, and many acquaintances. They are either Caucasian or black, but mostly Caucasian. I don't have close Asian friends and wish I would feel comfortable enough to develop close friendships with Asians. I'm particularly close to one friend with whom I share my religious beliefs. She was there for me when I was going through a rough time in my life. As a born-again Christian, I try to live according to Christian values. I care for friends and other people, and try to treat them with respect. I try to practice this value in my daily life.

The boys I grew up with and those I came in contact with were mostly Caucasians with blond hair and blue eyes. The boys would look at me but didn't approach me. It seemed to me that blond, blue-eyed boys were attracted to blond, blue-eyed girls. When I didn't have many dates, my parents once said that you'll probably end up marrying an Asian-American. But ultimately, I don't think I will marry an Asian-American, because most people I meet at work or in social situations are non-Asian people. I've dated black and white men, as well as Vietnamese and Korean, but I don't feel comfortable with Asian men. I think there's nothing that can be done to bring me back to the "natural state" of being Asian and enable me to interact with them. In dating, I think it's good if people date because they like each other, but it's not good if they date a person to make a statement or to spite their parents or to be different.

As for ethnic identity, I consider myself as Korean-American, but wouldn't try too hard to be either Korean or American. Until two years ago, I'd been trying so hard to be integrated into American society and to become

Americanized. That's really who I am. I was so good in upgrading myself, being the norm, wearing right clothes, right looks, all that stuff, to be acceptable to my Caucasian peers. Because I was so different from others, I wanted to be like everyone else and wanted to fit into my peer group. Probably that's why I'm so Americanized. But I was always aware that I was different and had exotic looks. Being a minority in America, I'm likely to be subjected to a stigma that people have, but I'll try to make sure that I am not discriminated.

Recently, when I came in contact with other Korean-Americans at a conference, I felt really proud of being Korean and looking the way I do. I feel I'm an attractive person, and I don't want to be blond and blue-eyed to be beautiful. On the other hand, I felt isolated when a lot of college students spoke in Korean phrases. I wished I could understand what they were saying and could communicate with them. I can't speak a word of Korean. I don't really know Korean culture. Yet I realize there is a lot of Korean in me; for instance, I like kimchi (pickled cabbage)—in fact, I crave it. I would want to learn more about Korea and Korean culture, particularly interactions between family members and treatment of women. I believe Korean-Americans should learn about their Korean heritage. Whatever they do with that knowledge is up to them.

I think I have high self-esteem, and I feel good about myself. I would like to develop more of my potential through academic achievements; then I would feel better. I gained much self-esteem when I moved out from my parents and became independent of them. Also, I gained in self-esteem, when I was able to stand up for what I believed and acted accordingly—even though I experienced a sense of isolation. In high school, peer pressure was great to drink or to take drugs, but I always knew I didn't want to do those things and stayed away from them.

Right now, I'm working at a business firm, but someday I want to study something like child psychology and would like to work with inner-city children, and want to pursue drawing as a hobby.

JENNIFER

(Age 23, Adopted at Age 3)

According to the adoption agency, I was found as an infant on the door step of an orphanage, where I lived for more than two years before coming to the States to be adopted.

When I was younger, we celebrated the anniversary of my arrival as a special day in my family. We all got together and decorated our house with Korean things and cooked Korean food.

One day my mom and I were talking about my adoption. She explained all the procedures they had to go through to find a child. I asked her if she had ever told me that I was adopted. She said that I knew I was adopted from the very beginning, but I don't think I realized that for a long time.

When I was growing up, I never felt uncomfortable being with my parents. I was so used to seeing Caucasian faces everyday and I kind of believed I was one of them. As a result, I didn't always see an Asian face when I looked at myself in the mirror. And whenever people made comments about my Asian looks, I was shocked as I hadn't thought of myself looking Asian. I thought all along my Caucasian upbringing had turned me into Caucasian, and I didn't think one could tell that I was Asian by looking at me.

On the other hand, living among white people, I often felt I was a very ugly, strange looking person. But, since I've been with many Asians in college, I no longer feel I'm ugly; I'm proud of being Asian with my dark eyes and my black hair.

During my teen years when some of my friends met my parents, they asked me questions, wondering what was going on. So I told them I was adopted. That was usually the end of discussion on the subject. Others asked me what it was like being adopted. Some of the questions they asked are, "Do you feel different?" or "Do you feel prejudiced against?" I just told them how I felt. I think they got some insight and cleared things up. And they understood.

In general, I'm glad I was adopted and live in the States rather than in Korea, because I do have a better quality of life here. After being adopted, I didn't have to suffer hardship. If I had stayed in Korea, who knows, I could have suffered a great deal of hardship or maybe I could have even died. I do feel I've been very fortunate, in terms of having a good education and having people around me who love me. I feel that my parents have provided me very well and did nurture a strong sense of myself. Also they made me feel that I am equally as good as they are.

My mom and I are very close. We're a lot alike in many ways—in the way we think, talk, act, dress or even walk. But my dad and I don't get along too well. I guess that is mostly due to the fact that I was adopted, rather than the race or gender thing. My brother, born to my parents, and I are pretty close, but he doesn't understand how I feel. But he understands the pains that I feel being unlucky, in terms of not having been raised by my birthparents. I wish my Korean parents could have provided for me.

Also, I feel a sense of loss for not knowing who my birthmother is and not having the language ability to go back to Korea and find her. My interest in my birthmother started when I was in high school. Then it sparked again after I graduated from high school and when I visited Korea for a week. Ever since, my interest has been growing steadily. About two weeks ago my interest became so intense that it was almost unbearable. I decided I had to find my birthmother. Now I'm going to different agencies trying to find or locate her. I'm determined to find her; I don't care how long it will take to do so. I just want to find my birthmother. I'm more interested in meeting my birthmother than my birthfather. It's very possible he doesn't even know that I was conceived. I don't think I feel bitter about that. I want to know the effects of heredity and environment on what I have become and how much I'm like my birthmother and how much I'm like my mother here.

When I see my birthmother I want to ask her, how she

felt when she had to give me up and if I can become part of her life. I don't mean to go and move in with her or to take her life over and dig up old bad feelings or history. But I want to be able to reconnect that part of my life. Also I want to know about her medical history and my family background, like what is my birth family's name and to whom I'm related.

When I talked to my parents about my desire to find my birthparents, they didn't offer to help me in my search. My mom said she'd be interested in meeting my birthmother, if she could. Although I think they never felt threatened before, now that my emotions are so strong about finding my birthmother and I'm actually doing that, I think they're afraid that they might lose me.

I've always been a serious student, very diligent and getting things done on time. When I was younger I liked math and science, I think I have a pretty good head for figures. But in college, I ended up majoring in English because I didn't feel I was developing any sort of depth in my character. All I was learning was about facts and "true" or "false." I wanted to learn grey areas in life. Since I became an English major, my writing has somewhat improved. Right now I'm studying Korean independently. So I guess language has been my forte. I've been a fairly good student, maintaining a g.p.a. above 3.00.

In grade and junior high, when some teachers or students held a little bit of prejudice against me because of my race, I didn't take it personally but I guess their ignorance made me angry. When I experienced racial prejudice against me, with racial slurs or some degrading comments, my first reaction was that I could think of the most horrible thing to say, but I always bit my tongue. I usually walked away and did not really challenge. At the same time I thought, "How lucky I am to have enough self-esteem so it doesn't hurt that much." Also, I was thankful for my friends, my true friends, who did not hold anything against me. For those who were prejudiced, I felt badly because they were missing out by closing themselves. I guess that by closing themselves away, they missed a chance of getting to know me and gain something. The other side of the coin is that sometimes I run into a few strangers who instinctively trust me when they see me.

In grade and junior high, strangers often came up to me and asked, "Are you Chinese?" or "Are you Japanese?" I was really offended and got mad, because it was such a rude way of bringing up the subject. When I returned home, I would get furious and ask my mom, "Why do people ask such a question in such a rude way?" My mom would say, "They were just curious, and didn't know any other way to ask."

When I was little, I hated sports and only wanted to play inside and didn't go outside. But in high school, I became very athletic and actively involved in a sport and learned about leadership. Some of the high points in my life were when I became the captain of our team and when I got a college degree.

Most of my friends come from a middle-class Caucasian background; others are Korean adoptees and those Koreans of immigrant parents. I used to date only Caucasian, but now, ideally, I want to date Korean-Americans. Some people I know won't date people of their own race, thinking that they're all chauvinistic or macho who cling to old Korean values.

As to ethnic identity, I guess I think of myself as Korean-American, because I was born in Korea and because I was raised in America and speak English as if it's my native language.

My parents and grandparents have always encouraged me to be proud of my Korean heritage. My parents sent me to a Korean culture camp for three times consecutively, where I learned about Korean culture—such as songs and drum dances. However, as I now look back, I wish they could have done more for me to have greater awareness of Korean heritage. I wish I'd done more activities with other Koreans.

It's really important to me to be proud of my Korean heritage. I guess the reason is again—if I don't feel proud about it I'm denying who I am and the country in which I was born. I guess the other reason is that it's a good way to learn about another country in depth. A lot of Americans are ethnocentric and nationalistic. And I am ethnocentric, maybe very ethnocentric, because lately the only people I really want to make friends with are Koreans. And everyone says, "You'll change," but I think I need to go through this phase first.

Recently, I have had a new awareness about my Asian heritage—after attending a conference which dealt with issues facing all Korean-Americans. Before that, I had never felt different or distant from my parents. My newfound awareness forced me to look into surroundings of my childhood and prejudice that I had encountered. As I examined the issues, I really felt uncomfortable and I guess I do feel uncomfortable now. I always felt I was ashamed being Korean, so it was easier to accept myself as American. I even called myself a "white" person. When I went to this conference, it really hit home. I discovered I had a lot more in common with these Koreans than with Caucasians and found myself connecting so well with them. We understood each other—even though we didn't talk about things. There were so many things we could talk about—things that we couldn't relate to my Caucasian friends. I met a lot of Korean-American men there and felt that I could connect with them, because they were raised like American just like my Caucasian boyfriend, but also they had other qualities that I realized I needed in my life. I really wanted to become more involved with Koreans and live my daily life as Korean. Since then, I've been trying to learn more Korean language, learning how to cook Korean food, being more familiar with Korean songs, and going to Korean church at school. I'm interested in learning about Korea—particularly culture and language, as I want to be able to act properly when I'm in it. I'm also interested in what drives Korean people, and what makes them to be materialistic and ostentatious.

My self-esteem fluctuates greatly from very high to very low, rarely in between. I think I'm born with a strong will that helps to enhance my self-esteem. Right now, I draw inner strength from my spiritual life. I look to God a lot since last year. My friends asked me if I had become a born-again Christian, and I think I am. I go to church and really listen to sermons, and I'm reading the Bible now. Everyday I look to God for guidance and inner strength. Before God, it was my family from which I drew inner strength.

My immediate goal is to finish my course for a Master's degree and get a job. Other goals are: I want to go to Korea in two years and spend a whole summer there and maybe study at a university with foreign student programs and learn more Korean. And I want to find my birthmother. After that, I want to travel to every corner of the earth and go to Korea at least once a year. And I really like to do something involving Korea, especially Korean-Americans and Korean adoptees in particular.

DIANE

(Age 23, Adopted at Age 5½)

When I was five and a half years old, I came to the States. According to what I remember, when I was about five years old, my birthmother left me in the street corner nearby an orphanage, probably hoping that someone would take me there. I think the reason she didn't take me to the orphanage herself is that she was too ashamed not being able to provide for me. Soon after she abandoned me, someone took me to the orphanage where I was given food, clothing, and toys. It was a Catholic orphanage, run by nuns, which provided well for the children. I stayed there five months before I was brought over to the States. When I came to the States, no one explained to me where I was going and why. After I had been on the plane, someone told me that I was going to the States to live with my new family. Then I started crying and kicking because I didn't want to go.

At the airport, as I came out of the plane, I started screaming and kicking again. When I saw my family, all blond-haired people waiting in the lobby, I was scared of them. Finally, I settled down with my dad, because he was the only person in the family who had dark hair. When he held me I stopped crying, but started crying when others tried to hold me.

My parents already had three children who were born to them. They adopted me because they wanted to have more children. When I first came, my dad took a leave of absence from work and stayed home for a while; then one morning he left home. I didn't understand where he went and I thought he would never come back. When he came back later, I didn't speak to him in fear that he might leave me again and never come back. Everyday when he came home, he tried to make me understand where he went. Then he took me to his office once a week to show me where he worked and to make me realize that he would come home at the end of the day. It took me a while to realize that they were not going to leave me. Also, it took me a while to adjust to the family. Whenever I got mad at them I threw things at them that were given to me. This was the way I expressed my anger, when I didn't speak English.

When I was growing up, I was surrounded by people who had blond hair and blue eyes, and we lived as if we were an all-American family. My family and relatives accepted me as an all-American child. So I wanted to look like my family with blond hair, blue eyes, bigger eyes or nose. But when I looked at myself in the mirror, I thought I was ugly. I was ashamed of the way I looked and never felt proud of myself.

If my parents had sent me to a Korean culture camp, I could have accepted more of myself and felt more proud of who I am. Learning about Korean culture was not part of our life. They never introduced me to Korean culture—such as language, dance, history—or sent me to a Korean culture camp. They could have done so, but never did. When they adopted me from Korea, they just thought they were adopting a child only, but not her culture.

During my teen years, I felt a lot of anger toward my birthmother, my adoption, my American mother and family. I had a lot of conflict with my mom and repressed much anger, in order to get along with her. She used to tell me how I felt, but never listened to or tried to understand what I said. She talked too much to give me a chance to respond. Then she would scream at me for not talking, "Why don't you tell me how you're feeling?" If I started to express my feelings, she would cut me down right away. Communication with her became difficult. If I didn't properly groom myself, put make-ups, or put on right clothes, she would criticize me that I looked like a FOB (meaning fresh off the boat and referring to Vietnamese boat people). By saying those things, she reaffirmed all those insecure feelings I had that I wasn't pretty, because I didn't have blond hair or blue eyes like most of my family or classmates.

On the other hand, my dad is an easy going, very nice guy. I have a lot of admiration for him. But when it came to my mother, he basically went along with whatever she said. That's how all my brothers and sister have been. My grandparents are sweet; I love them very much, although our relationships are on a superficial level. The only person I feel close to in my family is my brother who was also adopted from Korea. I call him often and talk to him, but brother is not same as parent, as friend is not same as family.

About three or four years ago, when I was a freshman in college, I came in contact with many Korean-Americans and started doing things with them. I felt totally comfortable with them because they looked like me. I can't explain the feeling. This feeling has led me to embrace the local Korean community. That's when I had big conflicts with my parents and started to have a great deal of resentment toward them. My mom was very insecure about my involvement with the Korean community. She didn't accept my Korean friends and the fact that they were part of my life. She began to put down my friends and also Korean culture, in which I began to feel some pride. I don't know if I want to identify with the culture, but I want some of it. I learned from my Korean friend, who is a second generation, that he had a strong caring relationship with his family and that all supported one another financially. The kids had tremendous respect for their parents. The family came first to them before anything else. That's what I admire. The family seems to have oneness as a unit, rather than all separate individuals.

Right now, I don't feel I have a family, as I don't feel love and security in my relationship with my parents. I'd like to feel close to them, but I don't know if it will ever be the same as we once were. However, I'm very appreciative of what my parents have done for me, when I was growing up, by providing me with food, clothing, shelter, education, and the best of everything. And I feel comfortable being adopted and living in the States, but my views on adoption have changed over the years. Once I held an opinion that race doesn't matter, but now I think that a child of one race should be adopted by someone of the same race. Also, I strongly believe that if you adopt a child from another country, you must expose her to her culture of origin and help her to gain pride and have curiosity about it. Not only that, you have to accept the child as she is, including her background, and make her feel she is as good as you are.

Because of the conflicts I have with my parents, I want so much to find my birthmother—just to know how it feels like to be with her, my own flesh and blood. All my life I've heard that my birthmother gave me up because she so loved me and wanted me to have a better life. But I have a lot of mixed feelings about her—a mixture of happy, sad, and angry feelings. I know that she was poor and had no means to take care of me. And I understand her situation, but still that doesn't prevent me from feeling angry toward her. I get angry, thinking that she could have persevered a little longer in the hope that things could get better. She had persevered taking care of me for five years—"Why didn't she hold on a few more years or another five years?"

Another reason for my desire to find her is that my

adoptive mother has never been what I wanted in my mother. So I want a relationship with my birthmother, perhaps not perfect, but close enough so that she'll listen to what I have to say. I want her to understand me, because I've never had that from my adoptive mother. On the other hand, I'm afraid if she might have a husband or a family, and wouldn't want me to be part of her life. And if she rejects me when I do find her, I don't think I can handle that—so I wish she would try to find me, the way the mother of my friend did. My biggest fantasy is that when she sees me, she would welcome me with open arms, and accept and hold me for a while, so I would be able to touch her, knowing that her flesh and skin are also my flesh and skin.

I want to visit Korea for a few months, hopefully next summer. I have to go, really want to go now, and experience everything there. My dad doesn't understand me or maybe he does. My mom is worried about if she may lose me totally. To me, it doesn't really matter now because I don't really have any relationship with them.

Throughout school years, I've been a good student, above average, and excelled in science. In elementary school, little kids called me names and teased me, pulling the ends of their eyes up in the corners with their index fingers. Kids would look at me and laugh. Basically, I didn't say anything at all. I felt bad and more embarrassed than angry, because they ridiculed me in front of other classmates.

In high school, most of my friends were Caucasian,

with whom I felt comfortable. There had never been times that I felt isolated, because I was "different." Some Caucasian guys liked me, but they didn't ask me out, because they were insecure about themselves as to what their family or friends might say. On occasion, I faced peer pressure to drink, but didn't like drinking. My friends didn't pressure me to do anything that I didn't want to do. Also, I stayed away from drinking because my brother who was born to my parents had a drinking problem, and I saw that his life was going down the ditch. So I didn't want any part of drinking, because it could ruin your life.

In college, during my freshman year, I dated Caucasians and at the end of the year I started dating Korean-Americans. I had a significant relationship with one Korean-American, with whom I remain friends. Right now, I date mostly Korean-Americans, but I don't want to get into a serious relationship with anyone.

As for interracial dating, if I fall in love with anyone, whether Caucasian or black or Hispanic, it can't be helped. I won't fight that. But my preference is Korean-American, because I want to have a Korean family with a strong cultural background.

My parents tried to influence me to date Caucasian guys. My mom didn't want me to have any contact with the Korean community. She believed that if I marry a Korean man, I'll end up waiting on him all the time and that I'll have no life of my own, except for cooking, cleaning, and caring of children. She's afraid of that kind of predicament for me. The thing is that she doesn't know me. I want to have a career first and want to become independent financially, as I do not want to depend on others. Then I want to have a family—strong family, but I don't want a husband who expects me to stay home and wait on him. I'm not going to be a waitress to him. In marriage, one has to give and take in "fifty-fifty."

In general, I feel proud of myself for what I've achieved, but there is much to be improved about myself. Right now I have problems with my feelings about my parents and my ethnic identity. Sometimes I feel sorry for myself and get low points, but I motivate myself by kicking myself, "Look, no one is going to do it for you but yourself. You can't depend on anybody, except yourself." When I want to motivate myself to finish school, I say to myself, "You don't want to be a bum in the street or cracking a little buck."

My ultimate goals are to finish my university education and to become prominent in my chosen field. After that, I want to have a happy family—and a strong relationship with my husband and my kids.

ALICE

(Age 23, Adopted at Age 6)

My father died when I was about four or five. I had two older sisters and one younger sister. After his death, my mother had no means to take care of all of us. And my relatives suggested that my mother contact the Korean adoption agency that worked with an agency in the States. My younger sister, one and a half years old, was sent to the States to be adopted two weeks before I came, because she had pneumonia and needed immediate medical treatment. I didn't want to leave my mother and begged her to keep me with her. She almost did, but she couldn't change the social worker's mind. And I stayed at the reception center in the agency for a week before coming to the States.

My parents adopted us because they couldn't have children. Having Caucasian parents has never bothered me or my sister, as we had become immune to that. Our multiracial family became natural to us. I consider my parents as my mom and dad. Whenever my friends referred to my parents as "your stepparents," I corrected them by saying, "They are my parents who raise me and I have my birthmother." My relatives—grandparents, aunts, and uncles—all treat me like their other grandchildren, nieces, and nephews.

However, from the very beginning, my parents and I didn't start out on our best foot. The first time my mom gave me a bath, she put my head under the faucet, and I couldn't breathe. I had never experienced that before. I thought she was trying to drown me. So I didn't like her. In Korea, I had never been in a bath like the ones in America, with water pouring over your head. I had other adjustment problems. I kept falling from my bed in the middle of the night, so I ended up sleeping on the floor. It took months for me to get used to sleeping on the bed. I had bathroom problems, too. I didn't know how to use it or I was too embarrassed to ask questions. Also, I missed my birthmother a lot and cried endlessly. Most of the time, I felt depressed. When my parents tried to hug me, I tried to separate myself from them, because at the time I didn't feel they were my parents or close enough to them.

Not long after I came, maybe after one year, my parents went to Europe to visit friends, leaving me, my brother and sister with their friends. When they had gone on the trip for two weeks, I cried all the time, thinking they would never come back. Their friends didn't know what to do with me. I didn't have the language ability to tell them what I was feeling. People in Korea and America understand the language of crying.

When we were growing up, my parents subjected us to so many rules and regulations as to what we could or couldn't do. For example, we could be in the shower for only so many minutes. I couldn't go out during the week at all, unless it was a school activity. I couldn't use the phone for more than ten minutes; if I used it beyond the limit time, my dad would carry me upstairs. I couldn't watch TV without permission and could watch it for only an hour a day. When I was thirteen, I began to have a lot of difficulty with my parents about the rules and regulations, which led us to a lot of unhappiness. My parents and I really fought a lot—mostly because we didn't understand each other. I thought I was independent because I assumed a lot of responsibility for myself, such as earning money from baby-sitting and delivering newspapers, buying my own clothes and lunches, and washing my own clothes. And I thought I was entitled to fewer rules and regulations. But my parents thought differently than I did.

In addition, being middle-class, we never had problems with food, but my parents talked so much about financial matters that I thought we didn't have enough money. Coming from Korea, I was also money conscious. So our money consciousness and restrictions put a heavy burden on our relationship, creating barriers between us and a sense of apprehension in us. When we were older we received a five-dollar allowance if we engaged in our family meetings, which we hated. Also, my parents told us that we had to ask for the allowance, but it was difficult for me to ask for it. While living in Korea, I learned not to ask things from my birthmother. Another thing is that if I asked for money, I thought they would give me up to others or a family counselor.

Everyday experience, like not having enough money and not having certain things, made greater impact on me. For a long time, I wore hand-me-down clothes from friends and neighbors. On the other hand, my parents valued trips and educational things. When we were young, my parents took us to Europe on a family trip. It was a happy time for us. We were privileged in that way, but for me, the trip offered little value even though we have memories. At the time, what I valued more was having enough money and enough clothes. In the ninth grade, when I needed a clarinet for school, my parents helped me find one through a newspaper ad, but I had to pay for it with the money I had saved from baby-sitting. Also, while in high school, I had to buy my own cheerleader uniforms and pay for my out-of-town trips. I know many of my friends had their parents pay for these expenses. And I wished I had more financial support from my parents.

My parents didn't really help me much in other areas, either. Most of the time, I was on my own. I got good grades because of my own efforts, not because of their help or support. I wish that my parents would have helped me with some of the conflicts I had about being Korean and being adopted. I wish they had addressed those issues more openly, and that there were more communication between us. I wish they were more affectionate toward me. I wish that before adopting me, they had gone to classes to learn about Korean culture. I wish they would have been more encouraging and supportive for me to learn about Korean culture or they were more interested or involved in it.

When I first came, my parents tried to send me to Korean school. I was six years old at the time and didn't want to continue because I really wanted to fit into American culture, as many kids do. Initially, all children go through a period of "denial" about their past. But, as I got older, I became more curious about my Korean heritage. But my parents had never given me another chance to explore Korean culture. They didn't seem interested in Korean culture or food. If I made kimchi (pickled cabbage), they turned up their nose and made me feel uncomfortable. When I was in the seventh grade, I and a girlfriend, at her mom's urging, went to the teen-group meetings at an adoption agency. At the meetings I learned about Korean food and a little bit of Korean culture. Also, we discussed about being Korean-American in American society. More importantly, I met other adoptees with whom I've since become friends. Being around my Korean friends and looking at them, I began to find them attractive. In turn, I learned to like my Asian features. I got myself straightened out a lot from that experience. But while I was attending the meetings, my parents made it difficult for me to get there. Giving me the ride seemed like a big problem for them.

From my adoption experience, I've come to believe that it's important for adoptive couples to learn something about Korean culture before the child comes and after that, to join a parent's support group so they can share their experience. In addition, I think the parents need to acknowledge the child's ethnic origin and not to raise her as a Caucasian child. In some ways, my parents denied me of the part that I am Korean. I believe that adoptees need to become involved with some kind of a Korean group which provides role models and peers who look like them. This will help them have respect for themselves and for those who look like them.

Since I turned eighteen, I've been totally independent of my parents. Now, I try to repair the relationship with my mom by writing letters or saying that I really care about her, and try to speak with her every weekend. Now, as I'm older, I realize that my parents had their needs and reasons for what they did, and I understand why things happened the way they did. I feel very fortunate that I am adopted. I know I was given a chance for a better life and am thankful to my parents for that. Now that I've met my birthmother, I'm even more thankful to my parents for adopting me.

When I was thirteen or fourteen, I thought about my birthmother once in a while. I didn't really start thinking about her until sixteen or seventeen. It was just a thought that I wanted to see how she looked. Then one day my dad suggested an exchange program that he saw in a religious magazine, which offered a scholarship to go to Korea. At the time I wasn't seriously interested in the idea. But the more I thought about it, the more my interest grew. I thought maybe I could learn more about Korea, because for a long time I had been so isolated from anything Korean. When I looked for information about Korea, I could find nothing which showed how Korea looks now. Also at this time my interest grew about my birthmother and I wondered if she was still alive.

Soon after graduating from high school, I decided to go to Korea just to see if I could find her. I thought to myself, "If I'm successful in finding her, it would be great, but if not, I'll leave it at that. At least I've tried and won't regret not having tried for the rest of my life." And I applied for a scholarship to an international students program and went to Korea to volunteer teaching English for a year. I went there with my Korean name but without my mom's name or her birth date. While on my teaching job, I met the director of an adoption agency who knew the director of the agency through which I was adopted. He connected me to the adoption agency, which still had my record. They gave me the names of my mother and sister, and their birth dates. Then I went to the police station hoping to find their addresses, but they had no record of my birthmother's address. So I thought she had passed away. The police went to my sister's address, but she had just moved two days ago, leaving no information about her new address. I thought that there was no chance of finding my birthmother. Then I was interviewed on radio. My interview was aired twice, but that didn't work. So I kind of gave up on finding my birthmother.

Eventually, with the help of my host family, I found my mom's address and phone number. But I waited about three months before calling her, because I didn't want to interfere with her life. Also, it was a very important decision for me. I knew if I found her, that would change my life. I couldn't just say, "Hi," and pursue my own interests and leave; rather it would mean my commitment to them. I would not have just one family, but two families for whom I would be responsible. Finally, I made the decision to meet my birthmother. When I called, I spoke in broken Korean, which was good enough for her to understand. I asked if she was the person whose name I had. Instead of answering my question, she asked why I was inquiring. When I told her my Korean name, she didn't say anything and just hung up. So I thought, "Well, this is probably not my mother," and that I called a wrong number. Or, if it was my mom, she probably didn't want to see me. I went to my host family and told them what had happened. They encouraged me to call her again, but I didn't. While I was gone, my host family called my birthmother just to double check what had transpired between us. After the call, my birthmother came over to meet me at my host family's place.

When I first met my birthmother, I didn't have any feelings toward her that I missed her, but recognized her remembering the years when I lived with her. At one point she became emotional and said, "I was such a bad mother."

I said, "You were not a bad mother. I love you for what you did for me." Then I started getting emotional, too. All the feelings I had stored inside me came up. Soon we were both crying. It was a moving experience. I couldn't believe that this was the person who gave birth to me, and that this is the person who has stories of my life before I was six. Before meeting my birthmother, I always felt my life began at six—because I had no pictures or anything to prove that I had my life before six—except for my hazy memory.

After meeting my birthmother, I'm more peaceful and content with myself, because I've found a missing puzzle about my life. Now my life seems more whole and together. My memory is no longer a dream but a reality that really happened. That puts me at peace with myself. So many questions I had before are now answered, and I no longer have to wonder about or dwell on them. That has really helped me. Now I can move on with my life. If I have any other questions, I can always go to my birthmother. I've also learned that my birthmother really loves me—the kind of love I had never experienced before I met her. When I was in Korea, she telephoned me every day. I really felt that I was loved. That's really nice to know.

Our meeting also benefitted my birthmother. At one time when she stopped eating in the middle of a meal, I asked, "Why aren't you eating anymore?" She said, "Now that I've met you, I don't need food anymore." Of course, she didn't mean it literally, but conveyed her meaning. She was filled with guilt, but now she is less burdened. So I think I helped her by making her more at peace with herself. Also, she knows that I've forgiven her.

Although they didn't actually help me in finding my birthmother, my parents had been supportive of my search. I thought that my meeting with my birthmother would improve my relationshgip with them, because I was away for one year and that they probably missed me, but in reality, it hasn't changed for better or worse. Some adoptive parents think that the parent-child relationship would get worse because they might lose the child to her birthmother. I don't believe that is the case. After I found my birthmother, my mom here appeared sad and probably felt threatened, thinking that I would stay in Korea and consider her not as my mom any longer. Contrary to what they may have felt, I make a lot of effort to improve my relationship with them. I try not to talk about my birth family or Korea, because my mom is very sensitive about that. I don't want to hurt her feelings or make her think that I'm turning against her and going to my birthmother. If I did, I know that wouldn't be fair to her. After meeting with my birthmother, I am even more grateful to my American parents for having adopted and raised me and for everything they have given me.

The schools I attended from grade to high had predominantly white students, with a few Asians. In the grade school I attended, students were mostly white, with a few blacks, and I was the only Asian. I was teased a lot about being Asian. Every single day, I cried and I hated it. I hated junior high, too. When I was walking home, kids would yell out of school bus windows, calling me "chink" or some other names. It was embarrassing. That continued into high school, though not as much, even though it was integrated with half white and half other races. I didn't discuss the name callings with my parents or if I did, I don't remember what they said.

In grade and junior high, I played in the band and sang in the choir, which made my going to school worthwhile. In junior high and high school, I was involved in the Honor Society and gymnastics. Also, I was a cheerleader for the hockey and basketball teams.

On the other hand, I never encountered peer pressure to drink, smoke, or take drugs because I was neither in a clique nor allowed to go to parties. Even if I was invited to parties, I didn't go—so I never met those kinds of kids who did those things. Also, I was pretty confident of myself that I didn't want to do those things, and I knew what was right from wrong. So it was difficult for anyone to talk me into doing any of those things. However, I was kind of pressured to be popular because I was a cheerleader.

In college, one time I took four classes and got straight A's in a quarter. I was on a dean's list for four quarters and I am on the National Honor Society. That's the only way you survive—the only way to be successful. If you're not focused, you lose sight of where you are going. A lot of my drive has been self-motivated, although part of it has been to please my parents. Sometimes my parents told me, "Study," but usually I studied on my own. Basically, I was motivated to achieve to survive and be successful because I believed I couldn't rely on anybody else but myself. From my adoption experience, in which other people failed me, I had learned to be dependent on myself. I had to be responsible for succeeding—so that's been the drive. I don't want to be in the situation—to be poor and without enough money. And I see education as the key to success.

My high school friends were all Caucasian, typical Scandinavian, very much like the family I grew up with, and also those Asian friends I met in the teen group. I still have contact with some of the friends I made in high school, but now in college I have a big group of Korean friends whom I met in the classes that I took. But also I have a lot of Caucasian friends, including my roommates.

Over the years, I have gone through phases in my dating choice. In high school, I dated only older Caucasian guys who were in college. I felt I could relate to them better because they were more mature. I felt some guys I met in high school rejected me probably because I was Asian. Also, they were probably afraid of what their friends might say. In college, after returning from Korea, I dated only Asians. The first Asian I dated in my freshman year was one of the few Korean students in the school.

With regards to interracial dating, I think we may face prejudice from other people in society, but that doesn't bother me at all. However, we may run into problems with our cultural differences. I think that what is more important is who that person is. If I were to choose my ideal mate, he would be Korean-American who was adopted, because we wouldn't have to go over certain barriers. Also, we already have a lot of similarities in our background and might better understand each other.

As to ethnic identity, I consider myself as Korean-American because I grew up on American values, but my exterior and my background is Korean. When I was younger, before being introduced to this term, I was told and teased about being Asian. Then, when I went to Korea, I was not labeled as Korean. They said, "You are not Korean. You are American." I was confused about what I was. Now I'm settled as Korean-American. When I spent a year in Korea, I made many Korean friends and ate mostly Korean food. Also I became adapted to some Korean values. So no longer I consider myself as "100 percent" American.

My self-esteem varies depending on areas. My experience in my ethnic group has helped enhance my self-esteem and self-respect. Beside racial issues, I believe you must achieve academically to build self-esteem. I get a lot of compliments from friends who would say, "I've heard you worked part-time and got straight A's. That's great!" They look up to me—and that builds up my self-esteem. On the other hand, I think that part of having high self-esteem has to do with having a good relationship with your parents and feeling being loved. And I feel my self-esteem is low in that area.

My immediate goal, upon graduating from college, is to go to Korea for a couple of years to teach English and learn

Korean fluently. Then I hope to find a job in which I can use my Korean language. When I come back to the States, I'd like to work as a flight attendant for a few years, using my Korean language. Eventually I want to settle down to a counseling job, working with adoptees. I may go on for a Master's degree, but I'm not sure right now. Also, to get married and start a family is important to me. I've never had a chance to choose my own family. So this would give me that chance.

Selected References

Brodzinsky, David M., Marshall D. Schecter, and Robin Marantz. *Being Adopted: The Lifelong Search for Self.* New York: Doubleday, 1992.

Feigelman, William and Arnold S. Silverman. *Chosen Children: New Patterns of Adoptive Relationships.* New York: Prager, 1983.

Girard, Linda Walvoord. *We Adopted You, Benjamin Koo.* Morton Grove, Illinois: Albert Whitman & Co., 1989.

Gilman, Lois. *The Adoption Resource Book.* New York: Harper & Row, 1984.

Jewett, Claudia L. *Helping Children Cope with Separation and Loss.* Boston: Harvard Common Press, 1982.

_____, *Adopting Older Children.* Boston: The Harvard Common Press, 1978.

Kim, Dong Soo. "Issues in transracial and transcultural adoption." *Social Casework,* vol. 59, no. 10, October 1978.

Koh, Frances M. *Oriental Children in American Homes: How Do They Adjust?* Minneapolis: EastWest Press, 1981, 1988.

Kraus, Joanna Halper, *Tall Boy's Journey.* Minneapolis: Carolhoda Books, 1992.

Krementz, Jill. *How It Feels to Be Adopted.* New York: Alfred A. Knopf, 1983.

Lin, Jennifer. "In–But Not of–Two Worlds Foreign-Born Adopted Children Are Struggling with Their Identity." *Philadelphia Inquirer,* August 30, 1992.

Melina, Lois Ruskai. *Raising Adopted Children: A Manual for Adoptive Parents.* New York: Harper and Row, 1986.

OURS: The Magazine of Adoptive Families. Bimonthly magazine published by Adoptive Families of America, Mpls., MN 55422.

Powell, John Y. *Whose Child Am I? Adults' Recollections of Being Adopted.* New York: Teresias Press, 1985.

Rosenberg, Maxine B. *Growing Up Adopted.* New York: Bradbury Press, 1989.

Simon, R., and H. Alstein. *Transracial Adoptees and Their Families.* New York: Praeger, 1987.

Tevlin, Joh. "In Search of the Missing Years." *Minnesota Monthly,* November 1992.